Networking in the 21st Century:

WITHIN YOUR COMPANY

Why Your Network Sucks and What You Can Do About It

DAVID J.P. FISHER

Contents

For Lizzard
Thanks for years of good ideas

Introduction

"**N**etworking — everybody has to do it, nobody has a good definition of what it is, and most people dread it." – from Daniel Pink's blurb on *Networking in the 21st Century*.

I wrote this book because I want networking to be a key ingredient of your professional success. Most people think networking only helps salespeople and entrepreneurs, but if used correctly it can benefit everyone... no matter your job title. Unfortunately, we tend to only think of building relationships when we are looking for a new position. Once that goal is accomplished, networking gets put back into the closet until the next time we need a job. But it doesn't have to be an afterthought. If you engage with your network consistently, you can leverage opportunities and overcome challenges more easily throughout your career. You don't have to be a networking maven or a "power networker" to be successful, but you need to build the right connections, the right way, and for the right reasons.

In *Networking in the 21st Century: Why Your Network Sucks and What to Do About It (Nit21C)*, I examine why networking gets such a bum rap. I start by looking at why professionals struggle to get consistent value from their networking. I explore the broad contours of what does and doesn't work in professional relationships, and I dive into the structural problems that have caused countless individuals to fail. Not wanting to simply focus on the negatives, I also offer ongoing strategies to make networking an integral part of your career. Then I translate those strategies into specific tactics that you can implement.

I ran into a challenge while writing because "networking" is such a broad concept. As individuals, our strengths and weaknesses vary, and we each bring a wide assortment of experiences, attributes, and skills to the party. And of course, we have different objectives that we are pursuing. Whether it's the differences between two attorneys with opposite personalities, or the different career goals of a recent college graduate and a Fortune 500 CEO, everyone's networking path is unique. This diversity meant that the book had to keep the strategies and tactics relatively high-level. I had to find a balance between providing information that would be relevant to everyone and tactics that were specific enough to be usable in the field. Because every networker has their own individual needs, I couldn't dive into the minute details that would apply to individual situations.

Thus, I developed a "one-size-fits-all" approach to the strategies and tactics that I explored. While *Nit21C* covers the bases well, I wasn't able to drill down into specific scenarios that different professionals encounter in the course of their daily lives. This is unfortunate because one of the most productive parts of any keynote or workshop I deliver on networking is the Q&A section. That's when participants get to ask for help with their personal situations, and they get feedback they can leverage immediately. It's where the "rubber meets the road". We connect conceptual strategies to the very real circumstances that people face on a regular basis.

You are reading one of my solutions to this quandary: a series of companion books that each focus on a specific group of professionals. I want to translate the strategies and tactics from *Nit21C* into relevant and specific actions that are applicable to your situation. I wish that I could write one for each person, but I don't have that much time! It doesn't require you to have read *Nit21C*, as it can stand on its own. However, there are ideas that we can't explore here because of space limitations, so I encourage you to go and get it if you haven't yet (admittedly, I'm biased).

You will still want to personalize the ideas from this edition to make them align with your personality, approach, and professional aspirations. I will do the heavy lifting for you; all you have to do is tweak what you find here to fit with who you are and what you want to accomplish. It's not going to do all of the work for you, but it's going to put you on your way to being a networking rockstar.

There's More Information Online

Networking in the 21st century is constantly evolving and changing. There are always new questions to answer and new ideas to explore. To stay up-to-date, visit:

http://www.iamdfish.com/companynetworking

You can ask any questions you have about networking, get my latest tools and tips, and join a community of professionals who see networking as a key ingredient in their personal and professional success!

Section I

DOES IT MATTER THAT YOUR NETWORK SUCKS?

Networking has a bad reputation. Even though everyone talks about the need to network, or that they should network more, it's rarely done with any level of enthusiasm. It's even more challenging when you work in a large organization and spend your days with the same cast of characters. How can relationship-building help you when you are stuck in the rut of talking to the same five people every day? Is it really worth your time and attention? It absolutely is; and there are important strategies and tactics that can take your networking from a "have to do" to a "want to do". First we have to look at why you've struggled up to this point, and we need to examine your existing conceptions, and misconceptions, about what networking is and how it can help.

What the Heck is Networking Really?

When people think of networking, they usually think of the company salesperson who goes to conferences to find prospective customers, or the recruiters who attend networking events to find new candidates. They rarely think of it as something that they can do as part of a large organization, especially if they don't interact directly with clients and the public. Most professionals equate networking with their job search process. It's easy to think that once you've got the gig you can sit back and relax a bit.

But that couldn't be farther from the truth. When you work for a large company, you open up the possibility (and need) to develop two different networks. There is still value in building relationships with people outside of your organization. That external network will remain a valuable resource. Just as importantly, you'll want to find ways to build connections to the people that you work with. Companies can now number into the hundreds or thousands of employees (sometimes hundreds of thousands). They have the same population size as small cities or even small countries. There is a wealth of opportunities that can be uncovered in this internal network, but it takes some effort.

Removing old ideas on networking is the first step to developing and leveraging this internal network. We have to leave behind the image of the dreaded "business card exchange". If you're an accounts receivable director or a customer service program manager, I'm not going to suggest that you approach your networking like a salesperson or recruiter. You don't need to go find new people; the relationships that you can develop are already within the scope of your own organization. Yes, it's going to require getting out of the rut of seeing the same people and having the same conversations, but that's half the fun. To build your internal network, you start by reexamining how you interact with the people in your current sphere of influence. A small shift in how you approach your colleagues and coworkers can often deepen and expand your existing relationships.

We are going to approach networking as a relational process. It's not just a list of names or a random series of transactional encounters. You are already in the middle of a vast web of relationships: the people that you interact with on a regular basis. Most people put little conscious thought into building these relationships. The goal is to make your interactions much more intentional. Ideally, your network will consist of a broad landscape of connections that have information flowing between the individuals within it. This leads us to the definition of networking that we find in *Nit21C*:

Networking is building a web of relationships with others for mutual support in finding business solutions.

Let's look at the components of this definition. The first is that your network is a web – and to have a web you must have many interconnected strands. Size matters. You'll see that there isn't a specific number to aim for, but a network obviously needs more than two people. When building your internal network, it's important to look beyond your immediate environment to the larger whole. Depending on the size of your company, there could be a pool of hundreds or thousands of individuals to connect with. Don't worry - you won't have to become best friends with everyone! But we are in a world of global communication and connectivity, and we want to leverage the opportunity to build stronger ties with the people who already share a common business goal with us.

Looking at the last part of the definition, we find a huge advantage when you are building a strong internal network at your company. Good networkers look to create a mutually beneficial exchange among the people they are connected with. Networking works best when you are both helping each other out. What's powerful about your internal network is the shared purpose that lay at the foundation of all of your relationships: everyone will (hopefully) be working towards the success of the company. Each person will have their own individual goals, but they will tie into the larger organizational goals. So when you help your internal networking partners, you help yourself twice over because it's tied to your success and the company's success. It's a positive feedback cycle.

If that's the case, why don't employees of large companies focus on building deep and robust internal networks? Shouldn't employees be clamoring to network with each other and build stronger relationships? They should, but there are a few obstacles in the way. Not least of which is the fact that most of them don't know how to network in the first place.

1.2

Navigating the Microcosm of Big Companies

One of the things we have to realize before we look at internal corporate networking is that the employer/employee relationship is in a state of flux right now. The work environment is changing rapidly and constantly. For a good part of the twentieth century, it was common and expected to work for one employer for the bulk of your career. My dad, for example, worked for the US Postal Service for 29 years. That's a pretty good run. These days, however, shorter work tenures are much more common. That's because employers are less committed to long-term employees, and employees in turn are more mobile. Combine that with contract work, remote work, and the renewed growth of entrepreneurial start-ups, and we can see the need to change our approach on how we conceptualize work.

That's a big, society-wide endeavor, but it has some immediate, practical implications. No matter who signs your paychecks right now, at the core you are the owner of a company called "*You, Inc.*". You are the president and sole shareholder. When you are employed by someone else, it's as if *You, Inc.* holds a contract to supply your services to your employer. Even if you aren't technically an independent contractor, the "employment contract" between you and your employer means that you are going to provide services and time in return for things like a paycheck and benefits.

The nature of work has also changed dramatically over the past few decades. I mentioned services and time, but in reality, companies are focused on results more and more. The rise of knowledge-based positions means that you can't just show up every day and punch the clock. The ability to solve problems and apply creative ideas to existing business challenges is in high-demand. There are very few pencil-pushing jobs because now we have computer-programs and iPhone apps that can push pencils for us. It's more important than ever to be able to leverage information and resources to solve problems.

When taken together, this means that you can't approach your work like a drone, just showing up every day for the next 30 years, punching a clock, and waiting for retirement. Reframing your approach to your networking isn't a feel-good exercise; it's a way to be valuable in the employment marketplace. It's important for you to be able to bring your knowledge and creativity to bear. Whether the challenge is bringing a new project to fruition or deciding on a new IT software package, your ability to develop and execute solutions is the reason you are paid to do your job.

But that still doesn't answer the question of why people don't network more. When you consider that some companies have thousands of employees, they should be fertile ground for internal networking. It doesn't happen, though, precisely because companies are so big and humans aren't wired for connecting with large groups. There's a structural tension in networking that stems from the fact that a large number of connections is helpful, but humans aren't adept at maintaining many relationships at once. We evolved in environments that encouraged us to connect strongly with only a few people. When we were hunter-gatherers traveling in small clans, it was much more useful to build tight relationships with our family or tribe. It's why we have friends in our department, but might not know the people who work on the other side of the 5th floor. We just aren't mentally designed to connect with thousands of people. In fact, the average number of relationships a person can maintain is only 148. (See my discussion of Dunbar's number in *Nit21C*).

It seems like an insurmountable problem, but the trick is to understand that you don't have to create intimate ties with everyone. In *Nit21C* we look at the power of "weak" connections as described by sociologist Mark Granovetter. His definition of a weak connection is someone you see only occasionally – less than once a week but more than once a year. Even though you don't have close emotional ties with these people, they are a huge source of opportunity. They spend time in different spheres of information which means they have access to new and different resources. For example, a friend of a friend who you see four or five times a year at social events would be a weak connection by Granovetter's definition. Someone you met once at a networking event and never engaged with again wouldn't be. You don't have to be best friends to leverage your networking relationships, but you need to have some ongoing interaction.

Developing a strong internal network revolves around understanding the power of these weak connections. You have a captive pool of possible weak connections all around you on a daily basis at your workplace. The focus of your networking is to connect with these individuals and develop ongoing relationships with them. There are many benefits to doing so, but you won't find any of these activities in a job description. You will have to develop the strategies and tactics for doing so on your own.

What's in it for You?

When I speak to audiences about networking, I ask if anyone has heard the saying, "It's not *what* you know, it's *who* you know". Invariably, the whole room nods their head. We all intuitively understand that connections are a key component to making our way in the modern business world. This is a big shift from the past when what you knew had relevance and importance because information was at a premium. But today, I can reach out with the smartphone in my pocket and search the collected knowledge of the human race. That's why it's much more important to have access to resources so that you can leverage and apply that information. Where does that access come from? By and large that access comes through the relationships we have. Another way to say it: *Who* we know gives us the opportunities we need to exercise the information that we have.

Just as the nature of work has changed in the 21st century, how it gets done has changed as well. The ability to connect people, ideas, and visions together is more important than ever. And the people who possess that ability are the ones that get ahead. If you think of your employer as a large machine with cogs and wheels, a solid internal network acts as a lubricant to help things flow smoothly. It reduces the friction that causes projects to derail, initiatives to stall, and delays to pop up constantly. It allows you to create new solutions because you can connect the dots differently.

This will make your life a lot easier and your business days much more productive. It removes a lot of the stresses that pop up on a day-to-day basis. If there is confusion or miscommunication, for example, you can call Susan in Accounting (or someone else you know) and say, "Hey, I got this email about the new policy, and it contradicts something else we have going on. Do you have 5 minutes to go over it with me?" That's a lot more efficient than an endless string of "reply all" emails. Instead of being out of the loop of company goings-on you'll have access to formal and informal communication channels that keep you in the know. Think of it as a non-gossipy version of the grape vine.

It's ironic when leaders focus so many resources on bringing all of the pieces together and then drop the ball on the most important step. Hiring the best talent is important. Having cutting-edge technology is important. Developing innovative solutions is important. But if they can't interact together, you can't leverage any of these resources. Relationships become the catalyst for creating forward momentum from all of the individual ingredients.

Take talent for example. If you put 10 of the smartest engineers in a room and they don't engage with each other, bounce ideas off of each other, support each other – well, you're losing out on most of their value. The basic premise of an organization is that the sum is greater than the whole of the parts. If you think of it as a math equation: *part+part+part=sum greater than the whole*, then relationships are the addition symbols.

This also comes with personal career benefits. A solid web of relationships in your organization can help you move up. You'll develop a reputation as someone who can get things done, not because you stay at the office late into the night, but because you have people you can talk to throughout the organization. You won't get promoted to VP of Marketing just because you have a lot of connections, but you can be better positioned for advancement because of a strong network. You'll get timely information about openings and opportunities. When you throw your hat in the ring, you won't be a random candidate that no one has heard of. In fact, you might even have a relationship with one of the people making the final decision. That can only help.

In the end, the more connected you become within the company, the more opportunities will arise, for both you and for your employer.

Section 2

CRAFTING A STRATEGIC
APPROACH TO NETWORKING

Networking will play a key part in your career…if you approach it strategically. There's a subtle play between good strategy and effective tactics, and when your strategy informs and influences your tactics, you will be more effective. It's important to know what you are trying to accomplish before you look at how to do it. I want to cover four different strategic areas that will help you become more effective with all of the tactics that we cover in the third section.

2.1

Investing In Yourself

The changing employer/employee relationship that we addressed in Section 1 highlights a quandary that stymies many organizations these days. How much should they invest in their employees? Because of increased career mobility, shorter tenures, and the rise of contract labor, employees commonly jump from employer to employer. That's not the best incentive for organizations to invest resources in their people. Why spend money and time on an asset that can walk out the door and down the street to a competitor? If they can fail to invest in their people, though, they are stuck with an ineffective and inefficient workforce.

Compounding this is the modern corporate obsession over numbers. There's a strong preference for anything that can be quantified. But soft skills, like the ones that drive networking success, are very hard to quantify. Even though the return on investment for building soft skills is palpable, it's hard put it in a report. That makes it challenging to get the necessary resources allocated for support and training. It's much easier to make a pie chart on a PowerPoint slide about something concrete, like the latest productivity software. That means funding will flow to these more concrete projects, instead of the less definable, but possibly more valuable, development of internal human capital.

There's also a fear that increased networking skills and relationship-building will lead to new opportunities outside of the company as well as internally. Companies are loath to build the skills that will enable their talent to leave. The path of least resistance, then, usually leads to under-developed skills and missed opportunities internally.

So if your employer can't be trusted to invest in you, who can? The answer is simple: you. No one will care more about your individual professional development than you. In *Nit21C*, I talk about the need to be an <u>autodidact</u>, someone who is self-taught. Go back to the idea of "*You, Inc.*". As the founder, president, and owner, it's your responsibility to build your skills. You have to invest in your own development, not only for your current success, but for the future opportunities that it unlocks. Instead of waiting for your employer to get on board, strike out and find the resources and tools you need to get better at engaging the people around you.

This doesn't mean that you should ignore the opportunities that your employer offers. I can't give you a blanket approach to the resources available to you because this will vary quite a bit depending on the size, culture, and focus of your company. The first step in developing your networking skills should be a trip, either physical or online, to your human resources department. Some companies actually are comfortable spending money and energy on employee development and have robust resources available. If you are lucky enough to work for one of these forward-thinking companies, be sure to take advantage of what they offer.

I've worked with many human resource professionals over the years and a common lamentation among them is that employees don't take advantage of the resources that are available. Whether they provide access to online courses or a structured internal employee mentorship program, there are often some powerful ways you can start your journey of personal development with resources already available to you. It can be as simple as asking, "I want to improve my relationship-building skills so I can improve my effectiveness with the teams I'm on. Do you have any resources that might be able the help?" It's like going to the library and asking the librarian for help with a term paper.

Whether or not your employer has resources available, you are going to have to take the initiative. Like any investment in yourself, it will take some time. You wouldn't expect to get healthier without going to the gym, so don't expect to improve your skills without putting in some effort. It doesn't have to be a lot, just keep it consistent. Dedicate a specific amount of time each week to improving your skills. Putting in 15 minutes a day, or even one hour a week, adds up.

Learn in the most effective way for you personally. There is no "right way" to learn. If you work best in a classroom-type setting, then find off-site learning opportunities. It could be a half-day workshop or a longer conference on building social skills. Often employers will have a reimbursement program which is worth checking into. There might even be an ongoing course at a local college or university that you can take advantage of. If you like to read (and based on the fact that you are reading this, you might), explore your library or Amazon for books on relationship building. If you are a visual learner, platforms like YouTube, Lynda, Udemy, and Coursera are only a few mouse clicks away and are chock full of professional development courses.

You might think that your schedule won't allow for you to spend time on learning and improving these skills. When your day is packed full of meetings, finding even 15 minutes in a week can be challenging. One of the best ways around this is to transform your commute time to learning time. Technology allows us to turn any environment into a classroom. If you are driving to work every day, instead of listening to music or the news, listen to podcasts or audiobooks. We consume a lot of information on a daily basis, look for ways to improve the value of that information. For example, if you have a 30-minute commute to work every day, you could have an hour of learning time. And that adds up fast!

Pursue whatever approach works for you. Even though there aren't degrees and certificates in networking and relationship-building, you will notice over time that your ability to interact with your peers and teammates will improve. You'll have to take the initiative and design your own development plans, so where should you focus your attention? What are the skills that can create these changes? Let's look at the fundamental skills that are the foundation of any good professional relationship: basic social skills.

2.2

Professional Relationships are Relationships First

n *Networking in the 21st Century*, I talk about the need to develop your social savvy. Social savvy describes a whole range of skills that allow us to build relationships with the people around us. Unless you are hermit, you aren't starting from scratch because humans are social creatures who live in a social world. Our goal is to build upon the skills you already have and find ways to deliberately and intentionally improve your ability to interact with others.

This is important for a very simple reason: All work relationships are relationships first, before the "work" part comes in. Whether you call it social savvy, people skills, or soft skills, building a network within your organization depends on your ability to relate to others. Don't get trapped by thinking that the org chart of your company will always dictate and define relationships. Reality is much more nuanced and complex. Your social skills, or lack thereof, have a huge impact on your ability to find opportunities and influence others. All of this starts by engaging with other people as people. In other words, you want to be able to make friends first.

In our hurry to rationalize our networking challenges, it's easy for us to think that only certain types of people are built for success.

That way we can think to ourselves, "Well, I just don't have the personality, so it's not even worth trying to build better relationships at work." If that's you, don't worry, there's not one single type of personality that can succeed at networking. It's just as possible to harness the power of relationships if you are quiet and reserved as it is if you are the loud, gregarious type. In fact, it might be easier.

This is important because stereotypes are mental constructs that often hinder our efforts. I once spoke to an attorney who spent most of her time reviewing contracts for her employer. Not a job where you would usually find the stereotypical "networking pro". All of her work was internally facing, and she didn't really interact with that many people. She shared that she was initially afraid that she could never network effectively. But her path to successful networking didn't require her to be gregarious and a social butterfly at events. She found that she enjoyed one-on-one conversations so she built her network by reaching out to colleagues for lunch once a week. It was comfortable for her and just as powerful.

So what are these basic skills that everyone can improve? Where should you focus your attention? In *Networking in the 21st Century* I cover a number of areas that are important for interpersonal communication. These include:

- Dress and Grooming
- Body Language
- Small Talk
- Sense of Humor
- Listening

All of these may sound simple and basic, and that's the point. They are basic, meaning they are the "base" that everything is built on. Most of the challenges that people face in their business relationships stem from a gap in one of these areas. Maybe they don't present themselves well or they talk too much and forget to listen. I had a friend who was a brilliant engineer and loved his work and the problems that he got to solve. But he was awful at the small talk that happened around the office, and because he felt awkward, he wouldn't talk to his colleagues more than was absolutely necessary. Unfortunately, that meant that there were a lot of unnecessary miscues and obstacles to getting projects done. To improve his productivity he didn't need more technical knowledge; he needed to be able to collaborate more effectively.

This understanding is important because the first step to improving your social savvy is to realize that it has an impact. Over and over I've run into people who want to improve their position and their influence at work, but they think fail to realize it has to do with their relationships. They usually think the missing ingredient is a degree or certificate and so they chase more technical training. Meanwhile, they make no efforts to improve their interpersonal skills and their careers languish. It's hard to advance in your career if nobody enjoys being around you.

Many professionals also cling to the negative stereotype of networking as "office politics". They're afraid they'll be perceived as brown-nosing or being inauthentic if they intentionally try to build work relationships. Office politics are mistakenly defined as disingenuous by those who are feeling left out or left behind. In many ways, it simply describes the informal interactions that happen on the human level in an organization. I.e., it's another way of describing networking within an organization.

The perception of office politics often depends on the benefits you're receiving from it. When someone else, maybe someone that you don't like, gets a promotion from leveraging their relationships, it's called *politics*. But if it happens to you or someone you like, then it's *networking*. So don't get caught up in the labels. Authenticity and integrity are important underpinnings of personal relationships and they are just as important in professional relationships. If you keep that in mind, you will build your relationships at work the right way.

Make Technology an Ally Instead of an Annoyance

For the most employees, technology is both a blessing and a curse. Yes, it allows efficiency to go through the roof. The collaboration and communication that are available because of smartphones, cloud computing, and social media were almost unheard of a generation ago. It wasn't that long ago when 56k was the ceiling for modem speed. You definitely weren't going to jump on a video conference with your vendor in Hong Kong at those speeds!

On the flip side, the avalanche of information and the need to be "always-on" has taken the rat-race to the next level. It seems that we have less and less attention to split among more and more things clamoring for that attention. It's easy to feel constantly overwhelmed and behind the eight ball.

Telling you to build your network by adding more emails, meetings, and social media connections would understandably make your head explode. But I'd be doing you a disservice if I told you that advancements like social media weren't an important tool, because they most certainly are. How can you approach technology strategically in a way that maximizes its usefulness without being exhausting? The secret is to find a balance to how you use technology to support your relationships. There isn't a "one-size-fits-all" approach. Instead, focus on integrating it into your existing process.

Technology is a tool, just like a hammer, paint-brush, or circular saw. Though you might be able to pick up a screwdriver and use it with little instruction, you might need a little help getting up and running with a mechanized jack-hammer. In the same way, there is a learning curve to using technology. So the first step is to make sure you get adequate training on whatever tools you are using for your job. Whether it's a new CRM system, an internal social media platform, or a new email response system, don't expect to use it effectively without training. I remember taking a simple course on using Twitter that saved me hours of time and made me much more efficient because I learned all of the shortcuts. Don't shortchange the time it will take to get up and running with technology. This is another place that you can use your company's resources. It's a huge advantage that you have over independent professionals. They have to figure things out by themselves, but your company might have a whole department that specializes in tools like social media, CRMs (like Salesforce), and other digital tools. This can cut your learning curve substantially.

In my years of working with professionals on using technology in their business lives, the biggest challenge has been adapting to the rapidly evolving landscape. Email wasn't around thirty years ago. Social media is barely a decade old. Of course it can be hard to keep up! Don't feel that you have to master every new platform and smartphone app. Social media is definitely a powerful tool that can save hours and make your life easier...if you approach it the right way so that it doesn't become a time-suck.

Social media platforms give you an easy way to maintain contact with the wide range of the weak connections that we mentioned earlier. Instead of reaching out individually, you can use tools like

LinkedIn, Twitter, or internal websites to share information and stay in the know in just minutes a day. In the next section we'll cover some tactical steps to take in bringing social media under your control, but in the meantime, think about the balance that you want to strike. Don't fear technology, but don't give it too much credit either.

Be a Profersonal™ Professional

What is a work relationship? What is a personal relationship? More importantly, where is the boundary between the two? As you look to build stronger relationships with your colleagues and peers, you'll find that the distinction between personal and professional gets murky. It's not a new trend, but long work weeks and higher levels of interconnectedness have made it very apparent that our relationships rarely fit into simple buckets.

In the 20th century, many professionals tried to silo the parts of their life: they created connections in their professional sphere, they developed friendships from personal interests and organizations they belonged to, they had their family, et cetera. It was thought that each of these segments could be separated and managed independently. But that never really happened. We got our brother-in-law a job at our office and had long-term clients that became our friends. The lines were always blurry. Think about how many romantic relationships started (and continue to start) at the office. That's the ultimate blurring of the lines.

When approached correctly, this overlap between the different spheres of our life is actually a good thing. In *Networking in the 21st*

Century, I highlight the power of a *profersonal*™ network, which recognizes the process of your personal and professional networks spilling into each other. (It was first described, and trademarked, by my good friend Jason Seiden at Brand Amper). As I mentioned when looking at building your social savvy, all of your relationships have the same foundation: they are relationships between you and another person first. Only afterwards do we put all of the adjectives on top of them (like "work" or "personal").

The profersonal approach recognizes this foundation. Compartmentalizing parts of our life might be intellectually possible, but that doesn't mean it reflects reality, or that it makes for good relationships. You should find it easy to increase the profersonalism of your work relationships because they already are profersonal to some degree. You are already engaged with your colleagues and peers beyond your official work roles. Every time you ask someone how their weekend was, that's being profersonal.

You don't have to be best friends with someone or invite your boss over for dinner every week to have a profersonal relationship. You simply have to bring awareness to the authentic connection that's already there. Focus on bringing more of yourself into your business relationships and connecting with the people around you on a human level. You are already in these relationships; it only takes a little effort to make them more meaningful.

Speaking of awareness, you also have to be aware of how you are interacting with others and where their comfort level is. Just because you want to connect on a profersonal level doesn't mean that Maria in Accounts Payable wants to. It's important to be respectful of the boundaries that others have set up. I know that one of the things that holds people back is the possibility of making a career faux pas when engaging with their peers. It's true that while profersonal relationships can help your career at the office, they can also hurt your career if managed poorly. Saying the wrong thing at the wrong time, or letting slip too much information can drive people apart in the same way that stronger personal connections can bring them together.

So should you just stay away?

Of course not! Yes, there is the possibility that you could make mistakes, but don't let fear drive your relationships. Do you avoid driving just because of the possibility of a car accident? You are going to be interacting with your peers anyways, and staying aloof can lead to just as many problems, without any of the potential benefits.

The secret to engaging with your fellow employees in a profersonal manner that's authentic and respectful is make sure that you bring the best version of you to work every day. If you are the kind of person that other people will want to befriend, then they will befriend you. It's common sense. If you are petty, mean, and self-centered, you will struggle to build your network. If you are friendly, supportive, and trustworthy, others will respond. That's not a professional strategy, that's a human strategy. Be the kind of person that the people around you want to be around, and you will have very little to worry about.

It won't always be easy to connect with everyone at work. There can be cliques and intra-office rivalries to contend with. Profersonalism doesn't make any of this go away. But it does give you another way of approaching the interactions and relationships that already exist in the workplace. Make people your allies instead of your adversaries by creating a strong base, and many of the tactics we dive into in the next section will be much easier.

Section 3

TACTICAL ACTION STEPS FOR "UN-SUCKING" YOUR NETWORK

n *Networking in the 21st Century* I cover twenty-eight tactical tools that can immediately improve your networking. As I mentioned in the introduction, I had to look at these ideas in general terms so they would be broadly applicable. My goal here is to narrow the focus and look at how you execute on the strategies we covered in Section 2. In this section we'll customize a few tactics, and we'll also add tactics that are more relevant to the corporate networker than to an independent insurance salesman or yoga instructor.

I encourage you to look at all of the tactics in *Nit21C*. And be sure to check out the resource page online for even more information to help you execute your networking strategies.

http://www.iamdfish.com/companynetworking

3.1

Meet our Fearless Hero

n *Networking in the 21st Century*, you encounter Bob the Hunter Gatherer and Bob the Accountant and in *Networking in the 21st Century...for Millennials* you meet Emily the Millennial. They act as lenses to understand the huge changes that have occurred in our daily lives as our society and economy have evolved. In this book you are going to meet William the User-Experience Project Manager. Bill isn't a real person, but he is based on many of the professionals that I've met and connected with as I have trained and coached people in companies around the country. Through him, I hope to show how some of these tactics can play out in real life.

Let's say that Bill lives in one of the Chicago suburbs and works for a large consumer-goods company. As a User-Experience Project Manager, he's tasked with projects that revolve around the digital interactions of his company and their customers. He's been in the web-design field for almost 20 years, including a few early stints as a freelancer and contractor. He's worked at larger companies for the last 15 years and has been with his current employer for about 7 years, and has had some career success. He's now solidly "mid-level" and has developed a good reputation among his coworkers for producing solid results.

He's looking to take the next step in his career, but doesn't know exactly what that is. He does know that if he wants to move up to the next level he needs to develop stronger relationships with the next tier of leaders, and he would like to have stronger ties with his colleagues and even people outside of the department. Over the years he has also seen a few projects fizzle or implode because there wasn't enough communication and information exchange and he would like to prevent that in the future. Ultimately, he would like to improve the amount of influence he has on his career and on the others around him.

He knows that networking is an important component for this, and that he has to build more internal relationships with his colleagues. But he doesn't know exactly what to do and where to start. As we explore ways to leverage the strategies and tactics found in *Networking in the 21st Century* and how they apply to internal organizational networking, we'll see what Bill can do to bring more contacts into his network and leverage those connections to move his career in the right direction.

Tactic 1

Creating a Plan

Before you dive into building and maintaining your network, you want to put a plan in place. Think of this as developing a marketing plan for *You, Inc.* Instead of making it up as you go along (and getting haphazard results), you'll want to outline a clear path forward. A good networking plan acts as a map to direct your efforts. Shooting from the hip only works in the movies!

Creating a networking plan doesn't have to be a formal and tedious event. It can be as simple as writing down ideas in a notebook or in a document on your computer or smartphone. If you have a colleague who is also looking to build their network, grab lunch or a beverage with them while you talk through your networking plans and answer the questions below. Be sure to jot down your ideas, though, because writing helps you clarify your thinking and gives you a reference point to come back to. There aren't necessarily "correct" answers to these questions, but the answers you do develop will inform and influence how you approach your networking activities. Once you create clarity around your networking efforts, it's much easier to make decisions about how to build your network. You will also find that opportunities pop up with more regularity because you know what to look for and will recognize them when they appear.

1. **What are you trying to accomplish in your business life?**

   Start your plan by defining the overarching goals you are look-ing to accomplish. What do you hope to accomplish by building stronger business relationships? The more specific you are, the better. It's one thing to say that you want to "build your career" or "develop more influence". It's much more valuable to say, "I want to become Director-level or the equivalent" or "I want to be selected to lead the new pilot project". You don't have to write out a huge story; even a few sentences will be a great start. This is the foundation of your networking plan because your end goals direct your other activities. For example, you'll find that once you write down, "I want to find mentors that will support my growth as a manager", they start popping out of the woodwork. A clear focus lets you realize when a potential connection opportu-nity is right in front of you.

2. **Who do you need in your network?**

   Based on your clearly defined networking goals, you should be able to identify the gaps in your current network. These are the people that you need to actively search out and cultivate rela-tionships with. Identify general roles or areas where you need to find connections. Even better, if you can identify people by name that you would like to add to your network, you can create a "hit list" of specific contacts to reach out to. Don't limit yourself to the obvious; dig in a little deeper. If you are looking to network internally so you can advance, don't limit your attention to only your direct supervisor. Find additional centers of influence in the organization and build relationships with them. It can be helpful to create a list of external connections you would like to develop as well. You don't want to focus on your internal network to the exclusion of outside contacts. No matter what your career goals are, it's valuable to have other people that you can talk to, share ideas and challenges with, and get feedback from. By actively looking to build these relationships now, you will get a lot of benefit in the present, but you will also have a solid network to rely on down the road.

3. Where can you meet them?

Once you know who you want to connect with, you have to connect with them. You have to put yourself in situations where you can start these relationships. More often than not, this means identifying the environments where your ideal connections spend their time and attention. Approach this like an advertising executive: connect the venue to the audience. There is a reason that beer and trucks are advertised during football games, and diapers aren't. If there are projects or internal teams that involve the people you would like to engage with, find ways to be included in those activities. Also, look for opportunities to connect outside of formal channels. This can be where the office softball team or an occasional happy hour can help. You can also be intentional with your social media work if there is an internal group that is active online. That might mean Twitter chats, LinkedIn groups, or active blog communities. Pick two or three places to put your attention, and focus on them for the next 6 months, because it takes a little time to get up and running.

4. How will you maintain and develop your relationships?

Follow-up is critical to your networking success, and it is easier to have good follow-up when you have a plan. Create a simple flowchart describing what will happen when you meet someone. Choose a way to organize the contacts you engage with (see *Nit21C* for ideas on how to choose a good CRM). Create templates for follow-up emails or messages that you will send. Decide who you are going to contact for one-on-one meetings and the questions you can ask in those meetings. You can also create a loose editorial calendar for your professional social media activity. That way you will know how and when you want to share content.

Bill's Plan for Success

Bill was used to creating plans for the projects that he ran, but it was still a little awkward to plan out his networking. But he knew it was important so one Friday afternoon he blocked out 45 minutes and took a notepad down to the cafeteria to do some brainstorming. It took a few minutes of staring at the blank page to start, but once he got started the momentum carried him through to the end.

The hardest part was defining his business goals clearly and concisely. He thought that would be the easiest part, but once he actually put pen to paper, he found it challenging to be specific about his goals. Projecting forward, he realized that he liked the company he was at, but wanted to move into a true leadership position. Up until this point he had managed small teams as they worked on specific projects, but he wanted to move into role where he would lead and direct a larger piece of the company's online approach.

He knew that if he was going to do that, he had to find some more champions in the existing management structure. He would also have to move beyond just the online department. The company was moving towards more integration and cross-functional teams, so it wouldn't be good enough to just get to know his boss better. He needed a broad spectrum of relationships. At the same time, he needed to do a better job of connecting with the younger team members – if he wanted to be seen as leadership material he had to find some leadership opportunities.

Luckily, most of the people he wanted to connect with were at the campus headquarters, so he didn't need to go looking for them. However, he did need to find a way to interact with them more frequently. Beyond the projects he was leading he could make a point to reach out to get to know them better, whether it was through short one-on-one meetings or just grabbing a quick informal conversation in the hallway. He could also reach out to a few specific members of the upper management team that he had already met and see if he could have lunch with them once a quarter.

He decided to use a simple task list reminder program to remind him to reach out to people. The company had an internal social media platform, but it had pretty uneven adoption. Bill decided that he would focus on using LinkedIn more consistently than he had in the past. It would allow him to connect with all of his colleagues, and at the same time, stay connected with his external network. He knew that staying current within his field would be important and he wanted to stay up-to-date with what was going on with his peers in other companies.

Tactic 2

Planting a Flag

t's hard to stand out in our noisy world. People are exposed to hundreds of messages a day and yours will easily get lost in the shuffle. It's important to create a strong personal brand that your networking partners can associate with you. I call it "planting a flag". If you can't be clear about what you do and why you are good at what you do, there's no way that your network will be able to connect you with opportunities and resources. Your message will degrade every time it's passed along (like the children's game Telephone), so the more clarity you create from the start, the stronger and more lasting your message will be.

The idea of a personal brand message is usually dismissed by the employees of larger organizations. "Why do I have to have a brand, people can just look at my job title to know what I do." The problem is: they can't. Companies have grown in size and complexity to the point where they are bigger than small towns in terms of population. You can't expect everyone to know what you do and how you support the overall organization just by looking at your job title. In *Networking in the 21st Century*, I talk about creating a niche that focuses on your customers. Understand that your "customers" are anyone you serve, they don't have to be external clients. They could just as easily be the organization's internal goals and your colleagues. For example, if you are in procurement, your customers are the other employees that can get the services and products they need to do their jobs.

There are four ways that you can start thinking about your personal brand. When crafting your brand, assume that your audience doesn't know anything about what you do. Even if they work for the same company, they don't think about your role as much as you do.

1. **Your mission—why do you work?**

   What's your story, i.e., how did you come to do what you do? Is there a particular passion that you bring to your work? What do you get from your work besides a paycheck? You can also move up a notch and talk about the focus that your department has. For example, maybe you are a part of the marketing team whose mission is to share the awesome innovations that your peers are creating.

2. **Your method—how do you work with your customers?**

   Do you approach your work from a different angle that can benefit your customers, colleagues, or partners? For example, I know a young accountant who is incredibly focused on using cutting-edge technology to facilitate faster invoice processing. It's a little thing in the larger context, but everyone knows he's the guy who knows about the convergence of numbers and technology.

3. **The demographics—who are your customers?**

   "Trying to be everything to everyone makes you nothing to nobody." That grammatically incorrect but incredibly sage advice came from one of my first sales mentors. Instead of being vague, be very specific about the audience you help, even if that's an internal audience.

4. **Your service—what do you do for them?**

    What do you do for your "customers"? What do you bring to the table that separates you from the pack? Is it your experience, your training, your passion? Be sure to communicate that difference to your network.

Bill the User-Experience Guru

Bill initially resisted the idea of having a "personal brand" because he felt that anyone in the organization who had user-experience questions would naturally come to him. And if they didn't have user-experience questions, then they wouldn't need to come to him. It was actually a conversation with one of his friends who worked in the legal department for another firm that helped him think differently.

His friend pointed out that even though she worked for the legal team of a very large company, she didn't view her job as a just being a lawyer who reviewed legal agreements and terms of service. She viewed (and communicated to others) that her goal was to help the company's mission by making sure that "all the i's were dotted and the t's were crossed". That's how she tried to make everyone around her more successful. As she shared that focus, more of her colleagues would come to her when they were still working on deals to make sure that things flowed smoothly. By creating a brand as the "person in legal who wants to use contracts to get things done, not hold things up" she had developed a great reputation in her firm.

Upon reflection, Bill realized that the explosion of e-commerce meant that he could play a pivotal role in the company's future. His experience in user-experience lay at the crossroads of the online experience for the company's customers. It would could be incredibly compelling if he became known as the expert who understood how to engage with customers digitally. He had a unique perspective because the projects that he had worked on gave him a lot of experience with how the customers interacted with the firm's websites… and how to stay connected to those customers down the line.

He would work to position himself as the go-to expert on bridging the needs of the marketers and product designers. His design experience gave him a strong technical background, and knew how to talk in a language the marketers would understand. He could continue to build his professional acumen around this and it was something he could share.

Tactic 3

Creating an Internal Elevator Speech

The much-maligned elevator speech is rarely a concern for some-one who does most of their networking internally, and that ends up being a huge mistake. First impressions are important. If you don't make a solid impression right off the bat, you probably won't get another chance. Your internal colleagues will give you the benefit of the doubt because you work for the same employer, but they might not be as favorably disposed to you. Also, you want them to know what you do and how you can help them. This won't happen if you have a confusing or vague introduction.

This introduction will sometimes be used when you are introduc-ing yourself to a room full of people that you don't know, which can happen with the preponderance of team-building and training meet-ings. It's just as useful if you are introducing yourself to a new project-team or committee. You can even use a shortened and informal ver-sion if you are meeting someone one-on-one for the first time from another department or if they are a new hire.

Here's the outline of an elevator speech that I introduce in *Nit21C*. When you are introducing yourself, it's important to remember that your listeners don't know anything about you. We often assume that everyone understands the nuances of our daily work, but that's because we do it every day. If I told someone I was a speaker and coach, they wouldn't know what it means. Or at least they wouldn't know what it means to me. When in doubt, err on the side of being too basic.

The Structure of a Great Introduction

1. Share your name, title (what you do),
2. Tell them your mission (or your main goal).
    a. Come up with something consistent (brand yourself).
    b. This is your hook—just like a song—so find your refrain and repeat it.
3. Give them a relevant piece of information (pick one – this can/should change).
    a. Here's a fact you might not have known.
    b. Here's an important department fact that has changed.
    c. Here's a new way I can support my peers and coworkers.
    d. Here's a twist on a current product or service that you might not know.
4. Give them a reason/way to act now.
    a. Talk to me afterwards:
    b. Reach out to me if you have any questions.
    c. Find more information on us from this resource (offline or online)
    d. Connect with me on (insert social media platform) at _____.
5. Repeat your name, title (what you do).

Bill's Introduction

Hi, I'm Bill and I'm a project manager from the user-experience team in the consumer products division (at Company XYZ). My goal is to help blend great design and technical know-how to ensure that our customers have the best experience possible on our digital sites. One thing that we're working on now which is really exciting is using mobile sites to engage with our customers and develop a two-way conversation with them. If there is any way that the user-experience team can help support your initiatives, please shoot me an email or stop by my office. Again, I'm Bill the user-experience project manager!

Tactic 4

Networking Above Your Pay Grade

You might feel comfortable interacting with your peers, but what about networking with professionals who are higher up the ladder? It's hard to build a robust internal network if you are only engaging with people who are on your level. You'll have to break out of your comfort zone and start to "network up". There are many learning opportunities that can be gained by bringing more senior people into your sphere. It could be in the form of a formal mentoring relationship, or even just one-off conversations that give you key insights into how the organization is run. It can also be incredibly beneficial to have access to someone with a larger perspective on the direction of the company, which can inform your own work.

Of course, it also doesn't hurt to have someone with greater influence and access to resources in your corner. The higher you go up the org chart, the more pull someone usually has. You shouldn't look at this as solely a power-building exercise, but it's useful to engage with the movers and shakers in the business. That doesn't mean you should focus solely on networking with the higher-ups, though. There's an important distinction between networking and brown-nosing. Remember that you don't need a network of strictly

C-level professionals and presidents to be successful. You can give and receive value from networking partners across the spectrum of experience. That being said, there are few important ideas to keep in mind whether you are connecting with the person in the cubicle next to you or Richard Branson.

1. Every person is just that, a person.

   It may sound obvious, but everyone is a person first. It's easy to get overawed or intimidated by someone's position in the company or job title. Remember that everyone puts their pants (or skirt) on one leg at a time. It doesn't matter who they are, they have the same human needs and concerns that you do. Relationships are built between two people, so connect with them as a person. I once ran into a well-known movie actor in a Chicago bar (think hobbits) and ended up hanging out with him the whole night. I think he enjoyed our conversation because I wasn't gushing over his movies; we just talked about the band that was playing and the city. It reminded me that everyone is just a person looking to make human connections.

2. They do have many demands on their time

   You have to be cognizant that you aren't the only one who would like some of their attention. Be respectful of their schedules and their other responsibilities. If you are looking to connect with someone who has a schedule full of back-to-back meetings, don't ask for an hour of their time or send super-long emails. In your interactions, be willing to take the first step and don't take it personally if they don't respond quickly (or sometimes at all).

3. Provide value.

   Go back to our definition of networking – it's about building mutual relationships. You might wonder what you can bring to the relationship if you aren't as high up on the ladder as they are. You might not have access to the same types of resources, but that doesn't mean you can't contribute. Take stock of what you can provide, and offer to help. Provide your perspective if it's appropriate. It's unique based on your position in the company. You could also offer to share your energy and time on one of their projects. It can also be as simple as paying it forward, and passing on the networking karma to someone else in your network. There are many things that you can add to the relationship once you look for them.

Bill Networks "Up"

After years of working in a large company, Bill was a little nervous about reaching out to connect with his superiors, even though he knew that they were the key to building his career. He didn't want to make any mistakes or miscues, because he had seen things go south in the past for other people. In some ways, he had always followed the approach of keeping his head down, which had a negative impact on his ability to create connections. If he was going to create new connections he wanted to build authentic relationships, because he didn't want to feel like he had to "sell out" or play into corporate politics to move ahead.

The first step was to reassess his relationship with his direct boss, Liz. He felt that they had a pretty solid relationship, but she had come in from another company only a year ago so he didn't know her that well. He decided to make a more concerted effort to get to know her personally, and made it a point to show up to the weekly department meetings a few minutes before it started because he knew that she always came early. It gave him a great opportunity to get to know her on a profersonal level, and it turned out they had a shared passion for jazz music which gave them a great bridge for bonding.

He shared with Liz that he wanted to build stronger relationships in the company to facilitate the progress of the projects he oversaw, and also because he wanted to possibly move up. He was careful to position it so that she knew he wasn't trying to take her job, but rather support her by doing a great job. (If she moved up, he could move up too). He asked her if she would be comfortable mentoring him in building his leadership skills. Not only was she happy to do it, but she suggested a few others who would be good for him to reach out to. This was perfect because he wanted Liz to be an ally in his networking and not feel threatened by it.

Tactic 5

The Magic Time for Networking

When you are looking to build your internal network, it can be hard to know where to start with the actual "networking". At least with external networking there are dedicated events like *networking* breakfasts, *networking* lunches, or *networking* cocktail receptions. When and where you are supposed to build your internal relationships is rarely as obvious. What makes a networking conversation different than a regular conversation when you are trying to engage with your colleague two cubicles over?

There is actually a secret for connecting with your colleagues at the office. It's hard to find because it isn't labeled and no one pays attention to it. This "magic time" for relationship building often comes disguised as other encounters. The easiest place to do relationship-building is in *non-structured, informal social opportunities* that occur throughout the day. This is a fancy way of saying that you should look for opportunities to connect with people outside of formal meetings. Instead of looking to existing channels for the opportunity to interact with your colleagues, pay attention to the times where you can engage in a conversation informally. These are often the places where you will be able to work on the profersonal nature of your relationship. One-on-one and small group conversations can go into more personal topics of interest than would be inappropriate for a committee meeting.

Many of these opportunities are already present in your daily business life; it's simply a matter of bringing awareness to them. It's valuable to seek out more of these non-structured opportunities to build stronger relationships with your co-worker; they can also be a great place to start new relationships. It can be hard to find a reason to stop by the office of someone you don't know (but would like to); but if they are on the same Sustainability Focus Group as you, it's easy to say hello before the next meeting.

A few places that you can connect with your coworkers and colleagues outside of the formal structures of the work day:

- Work Travel. You might not leave the office a lot, but if you go to a conference, off-site event, or to a client meeting with your colleagues, take the opportunity to get to know them. You can get as much value from the socializing on the trip over as much as from the official reason for the trip.

- Lunch Room & the Water Cooler. Relationships are built over food and beverages. The word "companion" comes from the Latin words meaning "with bread". Don't waste your lunch time at your desk trying to finish a report. Spend time with the people around you. When you do, don't get mired in office gossip or complaining - get to know the people you work with.

- Holiday Parties - Although there's the stereotype of someone having a little too much fun at the office party and doing something embarrassing, parties are a fantastic chance to get to know your co-workers as people beyond just their title. Talk about their activities outside of the workplace. If they bring their significant others, be sure to get to know them as well.

- "Softball" Leagues - Many workplaces have organized competitive teams, from softball and volleyball to trivia. Joining one of these teams makes it easy to spend social time with individuals from throughout the company. And since you've signed up for the same activity, you know that you share at least one interest.

- Pre- and Post-Meeting Chats - You can often get to know someone better (and get more done) in a 2-minute conversation in the hallway after a staff meeting than you can in the 90-minute meeting. Don't ignore the power of connecting one-on-one with someone to cut through the rigidity of meetings.

- The "Cube" Drop-In - If you make a beeline for your desk when you get to work, and then stay put for the rest of the day, you are missing out on a huge opportunity. Face-to-face communication trumps emails and instant messages. Don't be a pest, but take a few minutes to stretch the legs and have quick conversations. You'll get your work done more easily and build relationships when you ask questions and share information in person.

Bill's Unofficial Networking Approach

Bill's eyes were opened to the power of informal channels when he went to a day-long meeting at a satellite office for the company. He wasn't that excited about spending a day away because the workshops weren't that applicable to his work. During the mid-afternoon coffee break, however, he struck up a conversation with a woman who headed another user-experience group (albeit one with a different focus) in one of the other divisions. He wasn't even aware of her team.

And they didn't know about each other's work!

As you can imagine, they had a great conversation and we're able to share data and ideas. They even found some ways that they could collaborate in the future. Because the organization was so large, they hadn't run across each other. It wasn't the formal meeting that created new solutions, but a chance encounter over decaf.

After that, Bill recognized that there were opportunities that were all around him, he just had to give himself the chance to find them. It was the reason that he was going to his weekly meetings early with his boss, Liz. Their conversations weren't on the agenda, but they covered a lot of ground in those few minutes and he often got great ideas from her about new approaches to what he was working on. He also got insight into what was a priority as far as she was concerned.

He looked for ways that he could expand on that. His first thought was to take advantage of lunch-time to get to know his team and the people around him. Staying at his desk to shoot out emails to people probably wasn't as effective as actually having a face-to-face conversation in the cafeteria. He also had a number of team members who worked remotely, and he thought that it would be useful to set up video calls through Skype a little more frequently, instead of relying solely on email. And though family commitments made it hard for him to do things outside of the business day, there was a group that went to work at a local food pantry once a month, and he signed up for that as a way to give back to the community and meet people at the same time. These were small steps, but ones that could lead to much stronger relationships over time.

Tactic 6

The Politics of Formal vs. Informal Relationships

A n distinction to understand is the difference between the formal and informal structure of your organization. The formal structure is the org chart. It's the hierarchy. It's the described and delineated relationships between everybody in the company. It says who is in charge of what and who. And it describes how things are "supposed" to be done. That's not always how it works in reality, though. The informal structure is how things often get done. It is based on relationships, implied authority, favors given and received, and a host of other personal interactions and knowledge. Neither of these is better or worse than the other. They both have a role to play. There are a number of resources that dive into this very topic, and they are worth exploring. At the very least you want to realize that a good network relies on both those structures.

Many professionals work through the formal structures on a daily basis, and are rarely conscious of the informal structure around them. It comes into play, though, every time they ask for a report early as a favor or ask their colleague's opinion on their boss's mood before they ask for extra resources. It's important to cultivate your relationships and build upon informal avenues to get access and influence. This doesn't mean that you should go rogue and ignore formal relationships. It does mean that you have to be aware of who has pull and influence in different departments and areas.

Informal structures are exactly that: informal. This makes it difficult to give hard and fast rules that apply in every situation. There are a few key ideas to keep in mind as you navigate the informal power structures of your workplace:

1. **Align your informal conversations with your formal role** – Just because there are two different networks doesn't mean that you can work at cross-purposes.

2. **Don't make it personal** - One of the tricks to navigating the informal and formal hierarchies is to know what topics are appropriate for each. The line between the two can often be fuzzy, but a good rule of thumb is that if it is personal it should be dealt with through the formal network. Dealing with personal issues informally leads to gossip, accusations of backstabbing, and general mistrust.

3. **Make the effort to reach out** - People are busy. If you want to build these informal relationships you are going to have to put the effort forth first. You can't expect your colleagues to do the work for you. Take the time to reach out and start these relationships, and be sure to put in the effort to maintain them as time goes on.

4. **Know when to ask for forgiveness instead of permission** – Because there is a lot of fuzziness in the border between the informal and formal networks, one of the most important skills to develop is awareness: knowing when to pursue activities outside of formal channels. The trick is not to create more gatekeepers

and obstacles, but rather to find places where you can engage in activities that will help you fulfill your role and mission.

5. **Ask for help and give twice as much** – There's a natural flow to good relationships that consists of give and take. If you are just trying to "get" something from your informal relationships at work, you'll quickly develop a reputation that you don't want.

6. **Don't rely on the informal hierarchy** – Your informal relationships can be very powerful, but don't rely solely on them to get things done. A common mistake is thinking that you have authority and influence based solely on your informal relationships. But always remember that you still have to provide value and do a great job. You will rarely get a promotion just because someone likes you!

Bill Moves Past the Org Chart

I f was honest with himself, Bill would admit that one his biggest hang-ups in building his internal network was that he would step on someone's toes and create some bad blood. Even if that meant that not speaking up, he didn't want to rock the boat. It had kept him out of trouble, but it also had kept him from developing any influence or authority outside of his very narrow job description.

So he started looking for ways that he could build relationships outside of his direct line of reports that would still be respectful of everyone's role. He identified three people that he interacted with sporadically, but who he wanted to have stronger ties to. One was his boss's boss, one was the head of digital products for the company, and the other was a peer in the IT department. He reached out to these individuals with a relatively simple message, *"I know that our work has a lot of overlap and I think it would be great if we could schedule a recurring meeting where we touch base on the projects that I have going over here in user-experience. I was thinking something very simple. Maybe 20 minutes every month. Would that work for you?"*

All three said "Yes!"

The conversations were often short check-ins, but he developed a stronger relationship with each of them, and it encouraged him to reach out to other people in the same way. It came in handy when the marketing department looked into reorganizing their work flow. It was the same approach one of Bill's previous employers had done and it had been disastrous. Bill was able to let the head of digital know quickly instead of going through the different organizational layers (where it would have gotten lost). It didn't stop the reorganization completely, but it did alter it in a meaningful way. And later on it was realized that the original ideas would have been horrible…which gave Bill some important street cred.

Tactic 7

Using Social Media Internally

Access to technology is rarely an issue in a corporate environment. It's more common to be overwhelmed by the amount of information that technology throws at you. Combine that with the 24/7 access that technology allows (how many times have you been checking email at 11:00pm), and it can be hard to see how adding more to the mix would be a good thing.

Unfortunately, I don't have the silver bullet that will get your inbox to zero, but there are a few simple steps that will let technology help you develop your relationships over time. The solution for your networking doesn't lie in adding more items to your to-do list, but rather in being very deliberate with how you communicate. New communication technology can help you accomplish what is already on your to-do list, especially when you are interacting with others. For example, social media platforms can be a great place to build your reputation and relationships, but it can be overwhelming. Don't jump on social media just because you think you have to. A few things to keep in mind:

1. **Embrace change** – You can't stick your head in the sand and just hope for the technological revolution to go away. Specific social media sites may come and go, but engaging with each other on digital platforms is around for the long haul. The sooner you get comfortable and competent with these new forms of communication, the better positioned you will be for the future.

2. **Choose your communication platforms carefully** – You don't have to use every site to the same degree. In fact, spreading yourself too thin leads to stale profiles and missed conversations. It's better to choose one or two ways to participate with your network and then monitor those carefully. Let others know the best places to communicate with you, whether that's email LinkedIn, Twitter, text, or an internal social media platform like Chatter or Yammer.

3. **Schedule consistent times to check in with social media** – Just like you don't miss your staff meeting with your boss because it's in your calendar, you won't forget about your network if you have 5 minutes scheduled into your afternoon or 30 minutes on Friday morning to visit the different sites.

4. **Don't chase the latest and greatest** – Even though I speak regularly on social media, I don't think it's the end all, be all. In fact, in *Nit21C* I talk about finding a balance with your use of technology. Don't feel that you always have to be on the latest site or smartphone app to be successful. There are no magic pills so don't believe the hype.

5. **Leverage internal support** – There is a wide spectrum of approaches to social media on the organizational level. Some

companies are embracing it, and some resist tooth and nail. But to whatever degree your organization supports social, take advantage of it. Whether it's a whole department or just an intern, ask them for help when you need it.

6. **Share content that will appeal to your internal network** – One of the best uses of social is the ability to scale your communication. One message that takes you a few minutes to write goes out to your entire online network in seconds. If your main audience is internal, share content that will be relevant to keep them in the know. With large organizations, you can't assume that everyone knows what is going on internally.

Bill's Social Media Approach

For someone who spent his days making websites and mobile apps user-friendly, Bill was strangely absent from social media. He knew he should be participating online, but he just couldn't figure out who to connect with or what to say. And he certainly didn't know how he was going to find the time. There was a big opportunity to build a larger presence in the company and improve his reputation, but he didn't know where to start.

He went back to his overall networking goals, and that's where he found his inspiration. If he was going to be seen as an expert and a viable candidate for promotion, he knew he had to be "seen" first. He started by checking into the resources the company had that could support him (It helped that the social media team was located down the hall from his department). The company actually had a robust training program in which he could participate. After going through some introductory webinars, he realized that to keep things simple he would focus on using LinkedIn and Twitter.

As he got started, he decided that he would spend 10 minutes a day on his social media work. He put a recurring appointment in his calendar for right before he left the office for the day. He began by spending time on his profiles on LinkedIn and Twitter. He made sure they looked good. He was again able to get guidance from the social media team on how to do that. Then he started connecting to his network. On LinkedIn, he focused mainly on connecting to his colleagues at his home company, but he also looked to connect to other user-experience professionals around the industry. That was easy to do with his years of working in other firms and going to conferences. On Twitter, he focused on following authors and experts in the corporate marketing and the UX world so that he would stay up-to-date with the latest and greatest trends in the field.

Tactic 8

Networking with the Next Generation

The flipside of networking with your superiors is networking with those on lower rungs of the corporate ladder. These could be direct reports, individuals with lower titles in different departments, or even summer interns. While it is always good to network with champions who can support your career, a robust network has a wide variety of professionals. The corporate world is fluid and ever-changing. You can't know the future career path of everyone in your organization. One of your direct reports might leave the company and find a job with a consulting firm that works closely with your company. The junior accounts payable clerk might rise to become VP of Procurement. The summer intern might begin a startup that could become a new account. You just never know.

It's also easier to get time with people who are at your level and below. This doesn't mean that you want to exclusively network with people who are below your paygrade, but there's a wonderful opportunity to get connected to different departments and divisions through them. They can often have just as much access to knowledge and opportunities, sometimes even more so.

There is also an important opportunity to mentor younger professionals. A common refrain among experienced professionals is a desire to mentor and guide the next generation. You can help them by role-modeling what good networking looks like. This is especially important if you do manage other people, because they will learn how to network from you. If you want them to build successful relationships within the company, they need exposure to the right way to do it.

There are few key guidelines to building relationships outside of formal channels with less senior colleagues. Keep these in mind and you'll be okay.

- **Create a two-way street** - Good networking is based on reciprocity of information and help. Help foster a strong relationship by both giving and accepting help. Even if it's just information and feedback that is going both ways, that back and forth is more important than you just sharing your resources. And everyone has something to offer. Reread Tactic 4 on **Networking Above Your Paygrade**, and flip the script if you are the one in the position of authority.

- **Don't intimidate or bully with your position** - It can be easy (if unintentional) to put someone in an awkward position when they are lower in the organizational hierarchy. It's possible that they might feel forced to network with you because of your position. The trick is to be aware and always give an out.

- **Be straightforward about what you can or will do** - It's also easy to make someone think that you can help them in ways that you can't, especially when trying to build relationships and make the other person like us. Create clear boundaries about what kind of support you can give the other person.

Bill Makes New Friends

There were a lot of opportunities for Bill to network with younger professionals – the digital world was a young field and sometimes he felt like the oldest guy in the room (he was convinced he was the only one on his team who still remembered the awful noise that original phone modems made). It was still a shift for him to think about networking with those lower down the corporate ladder. He had always thought about networking as something you did with the movers and shakers.

The first place for him to look was within his own department. He realized that there were a lot of chances to get to know his younger colleagues that he hadn't been open to in the past. He didn't have to know who was playing Lollapalooza or be hip, he just had to be open to making human connections. He also invited some the younger team members to join him for lunch every once in a while in the cafeteria – and then he made a point to get to know about them instead of just talking about their current project.

He was rewarded with a wealth of information. Not only did he get to know them better, but as they became more comfortable with him, they were more likely to share some of their ideas informally. It turned out that they had some pretty good ideas. Six months down the line, one of the young contractors that had worked with the digital team found a permanent position in the general marketing division. That came into play when she became the point of contact for the biggest project Bill had ever led. It further opened his eyes to the non-linear nature of relationships and the value of connecting with a broad range of people.

Tactic 9

Balancing Internal and External Networking

Most of this book is focused on building your internal network. It's important to remember, though, that you can't ignore your external network. The different networks play different roles in your career development, and you need to pay attention to both. Most of *Nit21C* is focused on external networking, and you can find a wealth of information there. You will want to build these networks in parallel, and it can be a bit of a balancing act, especially when you have a finite amount of time.

Focused internal networks are important to your career because they have access to the information and news that you need. If your employer is a self-contained community, the resources and information you need are going to be accessed through your internal relationships. You need to be able to stay in the loop. But if you are only networking internally, it's easy to have career "blinders" on. You can fall into a parochial perspective when you only spend time with people that think like you; and that can grow stale. You miss out on different contexts and ideas. It's not that the perspective of your internal network is bad, it's just that it's limited.

Diffuse external networks are the opposite of focused ones. Instead of building a web of connections in the same just in your company, you branch out and create relationships with people in a variety of roles and industries. It can make sense to connect with colleagues in the same industry but at different companies, but it can also help to engage with people in total different fields. Different perspectives offer "lateral thinking" which introduces new ways to solve problems. And you never know who your diffuse network is connected to. They spend their time in very different social circles and might have access to just the person you need.

Both of these networks feed different aspects of your career. To find success, balance your attention and time between the two of them. A valuable connection strategy will weave your internal and external network into a unified whole, one that provides a wealth of resources to help you grow your career.

1. **Join functional organizations** - Look for external networking events that are in your field. One of the best ways to build your external network is to connect with others who are in the same field but at other companies. You don't have to view them as competition, but rather as fellow practitioners.

2. **Build your reputation externally to support your internal credibility** - One of the best ways to build your credibility internally is to have outside actors bolster your reputation. For example, I know a vice president who was interviewed in a leading industry magazine. It gave her a lot of internal recognition, and when she shared it on social media, it went "viral" within her company.

3. **Look to blend the two networks** - Create opportunities to combine your networks. You can take your co-workers to networking events in your areas. You can also make introductions between people who work with your company

and others that work in their field from other organizations. Become a bridge between the two worlds and you will prove how valuable you are.

4. **Use social media** – Staying connected to all of your connections easily and efficiently is where social media shines. Whatever platforms you are using, assume that you are going to have both an internal and external audience listening. Even when you are posting information that has mostly an internal focus, the rest of your network can pay attention. You can share your brand, and your company's brand, without much extra effort.

Bill Builds Both Internal and External Credibility

B ill already had the beginnings of a solid external network, but he hadn't done much to maintain it over the years. He had a smattering of contacts and business cards from past jobs and a few conferences he had attended over the years, but it didn't amount to much. He wanted to see if there was a way he could build both of his networks at the same time. If they could feed into each other, he could leverage his knowledge and credibility externally to build his internal reputation, and vice versa.

He decided to use his new focus on social media to help bridge both of these networks. He had been hesitant to connect with his coworkers on LinkedIn because he didn't think there was a reason. Now he saw that he could share what he was working on in the user-experience world with both his internal and external network. He also made a deliberate attempt to reconnect online with past colleagues so that he could stay in touch. He hadn't before because he thought it would make it appear that he was looking for a new job, but now he wanted to use it to stay in the know about the trends in the industry.

He also re-upped his membership in the Chicago chapter of the User-Experience Professionals Association. He invited two of the other project leads at the company to join as well. And when he went to the meetings, he made sure to bring one of the younger team members with him. That allowed him to connect his team into the industry and they brought that back into their daily work. It also helped his stature in the department.

His credibility was also boosted when he was interviewed for a well-known digital media podcast, which actually led to a few other podcast appearances. He shared that throughout his LinkedIn network and on Twitter. It was picked up by the company newsletter and that went a long way to increasing his visibility with the higher-ups. He also met a number of vendors at association meetings, and was able to make a recommendation to one of the other department heads when they were looking to change their cloud computing provider. That's when he realized that networking was helping him… even though he wasn't in the sales department!

Tactic 10

Connect These Tactics to Your Larger Goals

W e've only unpacked a few of the tactics that in *Networking in the 21st Century*, but you now have a solid foundation for moving forward. There's twenty eight more than you can still dive into! The most important thing to remember when networking: Be intentional. Too often, professionals throw their networking energy around willy-nilly, and have little to see for it. Haphazard networking creates haphazard results. At the beginning of the book, we looked at a simple definition of networking:

"Networking is building a web of relationships with others for mutual support in finding business solutions."

We started with that definition because I wanted you to be able to connect the strategies and tactics we looked at with your overall networking goals. It's the same reason we started the tactics section by creating a networking plan: it helps to create a framework for all of your activity. My goal in writing this book was to connect a few of the strategies and tactics I cover in *Nit21C* to the real-life scenarios that we all face as we build our business relationships. It's not meant to be comprehensive, but rather it's designed to give you a place to start your journey.

To understand the larger context on why you've been struggling to build your network up to this point, I encourage you to get a copy of *Nit21C* (it'll be worth it, I promise). More importantly, you'll also find more information there on how to improve your network, including key strategies such as:

1. Learning how you can succeed at networking whether you are an extrovert or an introvert.
2. Finding out about the key role that personal development plays in your networking.
3. Understanding how your brain is wired to work against building a large network and how to change your approach to set yourself up for success.

You'll also learn more tactics, including how to:

1. Have a conversation with anyone, anytime.
2. Network with your competition.
3. Reach out to ask for help comfortably and easily.
4. Ask questions to uncover new business opportunities.
5. Begin and end conversations at events.

Concluding Thoughts

When I speak to audiences, I often finish by showing a picture of a field of ripe wheat, and I talk about the approach that farmers take to growing crops. They don't plant a seed and then come back the next day expecting full-grown plants. They understand that it's a process that starts with the seeds, but requires cultivation and attention over time to see the true benefits.

Reading about networking without taking action would be like a farmer reading about growing crops. It doesn't create results by itself. You have to take action. You have to plant seeds and then nourish what you've planted. You have an advantage because you are already in the midst of a fertile field of people to engage with. You just need the faith of the farmer who knows that there will be a payoff in the end. The more effort you put in now, the more rewards you can reap in the future.

So now it's back on you – what are you going to do with this information? The fate of your career now, and in the future, is in your hands. There are many things in life and business that you don't control, but your activities are one of things that you do. I wish you the best of luck.

Happy Networking!

Additional Resources

You can get your print, digital, or audio copy of *Networking in the 21st Century: Why Your Network Sucks and What to Do About It* on Amazon.com.

Visit the exclusive home page for the readers of this book at:

www.iamdfish.com/companynetworking

It's full of tools and tips for making networking a valuable part of your professional life. I regularly update it and if you have any questions for me, or networking ideas that I missed, I'd love to hear from you!

About the Author

David J.P. Fisher lives in Evanston, Illinois, next to a beautiful cemetery, which acts as a reminder every morning to not take life for granted (and be on the lookout for zombies). He is an entrepreneur, coach, salesman, writer, meditator, marketer, musician, son, friend, brother, slam poet, clairvoyant, comedian, salsa dancer, lover of life, teller of bad jokes, yoga enthusiast, and an average cook—as long as it's pancakes or hummus.

Known as D. Fish to everyone (except his mom), he is a sought-after speaker, author, and business coach. His first full-length book, *Networking in the 21st Century: Why Your Network Sucks and What to Do About It* was an Amazon best-seller. His passion for growth and development has allowed him to influence thousands of others during his professional career. As the current president of RockStar Consulting, he helps individuals become RockStars both offline and online by building their networking, sales, and entrepreneurial skills.

You can find him online at all the usual places:

Website: www.iamdfish.com
Linkedin: www.linkedin.com/in/iamdfish
Twitter: @dfishrockstar

Stop by and say hello!

Acknowledgements

The first thank you as always goes to you the reader. There are a lot of things you could do with your time, and I'm honored that you gave me a bit of your attention.

This book got its start in a conversation with my friend Liz at a local coffeeshop, once again proving the value of having really smart people in your network.

Debbie O'Byrne, you created yet another awesome cover.

Colette, Chrissie, Amy, Rob, Brian, Joe, and all of my other friends continue to be the best network ever!

And I won't get tired of saying it, so once again, I have to thank Helen for choosing me as her person and putting up with my early morning writing sessions.

www.ingramcontent.com/pod-product-compliance
Lightning Source LLC
Chambersburg PA
CBHW031729210326
41520CB00042B/1504